For REBECCA

Thanks to Mrs. Mills
and her first-grade class,
Community Park School, Princeton, New Jersey

ISBN 0-590-13201-6

12 11 10 9 8 7 6 5 4 3   9/9 0 1/0

                                                                    14
Printed in the U.S.A.

Contents

Fraction Action   4

Get Ready, Get Set   11

A Fair Share   16

Lemonade for Sale   22

Teacher's Test   28

Answers   32

FRACTION ACTION

One morning, Miss Prime turned off all the lights in the classroom.

Okay, everybody, watch the screen, and you'll see how to draw a fraction.

Start with a WHOLE shape.

Then make it into two equal parts.

Each part is called ONE HALF.

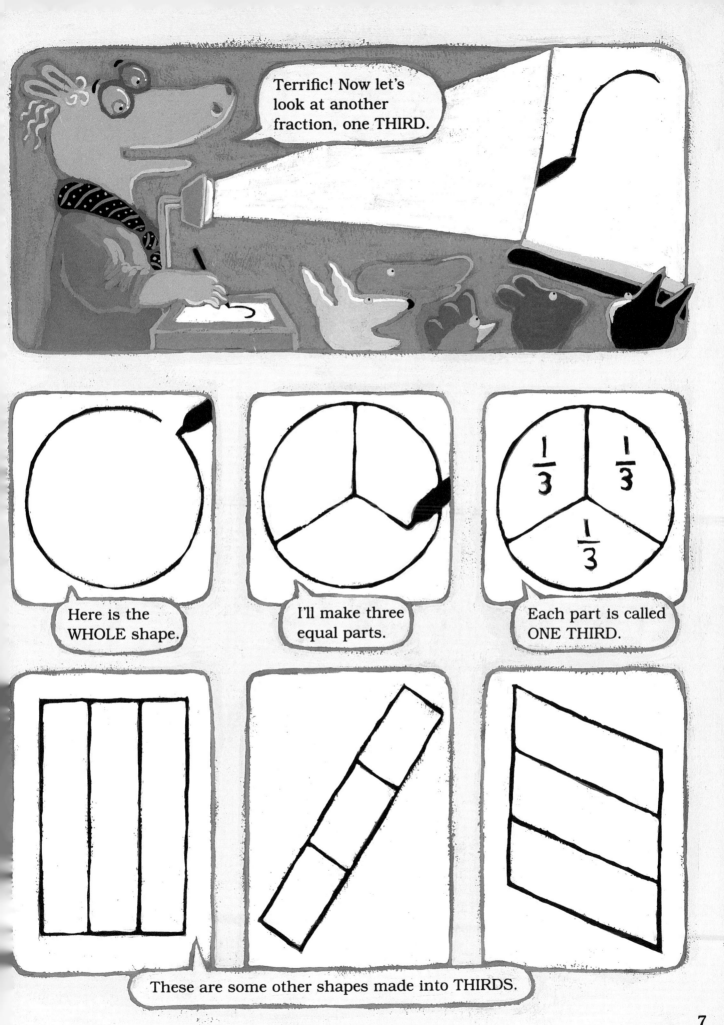

Terrific! Now let's look at another fraction, one THIRD.

Here is the WHOLE shape.

I'll make three equal parts.

Each part is called ONE THIRD.

$\frac{1}{3}$ $\frac{1}{3}$ $\frac{1}{3}$

These are some other shapes made into THIRDS.

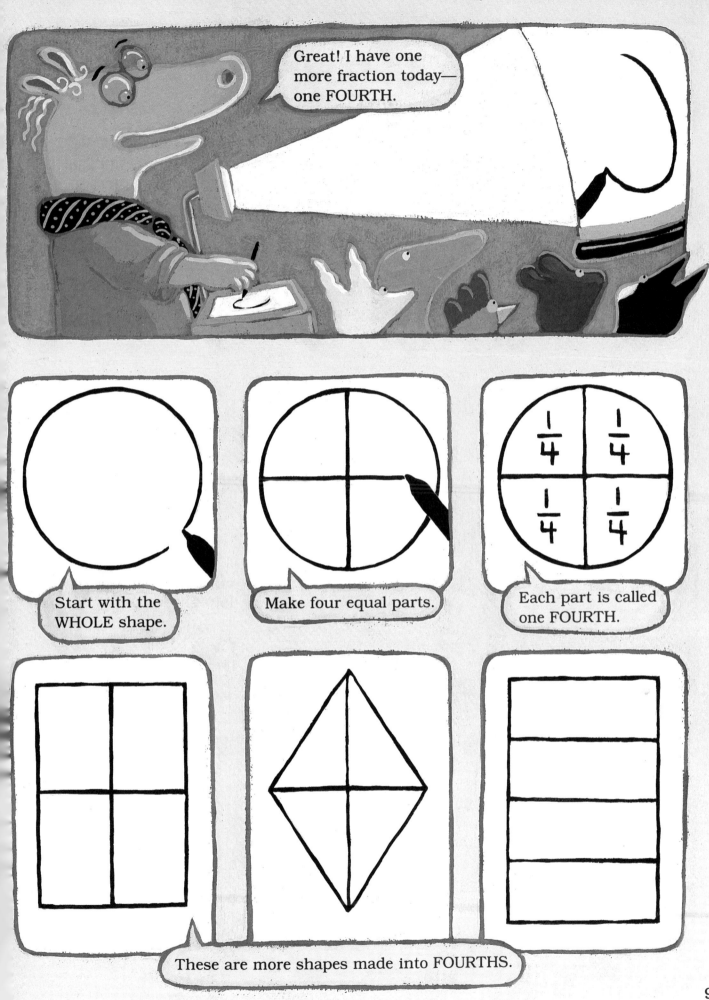

GeT ReAdy, GeT SeT

A few days later, Miss Prime turned out the lights again.

12

13

14

A Fair ShAr

One Saturday at about noon, Sadie heard a loud knock at the door.

17

What fractions were used to make lunch? (Hint: there were 3 different fractions.) See page 32.

Lemonade For Sale

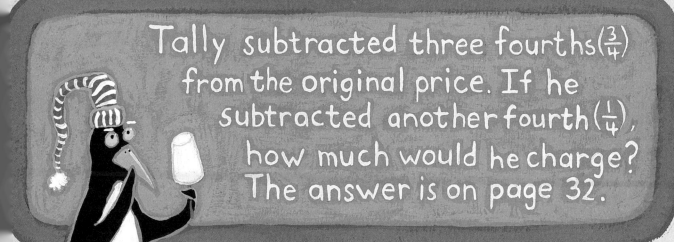

Tally subtracted three fourths($\frac{3}{4}$) from the original price. If he subtracted another fourth($\frac{1}{4}$), how much would he charge? The answer is on page 32.

TEACHER'S TEST

Miss Prime tapped her desk with a ruler.

29

What fraction of Miss Prime's students is Ginger? (Answer is on next page.)

Answers

page 10: The smallest fraction is ONE FOURTH.

page 15: There were 30 marbles in the whole set.

page 21: The fractions used to make lunch were:

 ONE HALF ($\frac{1}{2}$), to slice the oranges

 ONE FOURTH ($\frac{1}{4}$), to cut the watermelon

ONE FIFTH ($\frac{1}{5}$), to divide the fruit salad

page 27: If Tally subtracted another ONE FOURTH ($\frac{1}{4}$) from the original price, he would be charging zero.

page 31: Ginger is ONE FIFTH ($\frac{1}{5}$) of the set of Miss Prime's students.